⌒ LIGHT WAS EVERYWHERE ⌒

January 2011

Happy
Joyous
Wonderful
Birth
Day

with love
Donna & Bob

LIGHT
WAS
EVERYWHERE

POETRY BY

RICHARD WEHRMAN

 GOLDENSTONE PRESS | *Benson, North Carolina*

MERLINWOOD BOOKS ○ *East Bloomfield, New York*

Published by Goldenstone Press and Merlinwood Books

Goldsenstone Press
P.O. Box 7
Benson, North Carolina 27504
www.goldenstonepress.com

Merlinwood Books
P.O. Box 146
E. Bloomfield, New York 14443

ISBN: 978-0-9832261-1-6

Book design by Richard Wehrman, www.merlinwood.net
Mandala, *Heart Presence*, page 59, by Richard Wehrman

"Half Light", "Love for Sale", "Saturation Point", and "We Are Sailors" also appeared in *Heartwork–How To Get What You Really, Really Want* by Dale L. Goldstein (Heartwork Institute Inc., 2007)

GOLDENSTONE PRESS

Goldenstone Press seeks to make original spiritual thought available as a force of individual, cultural, and world revitalization. The press is an integral dimension of the work of the School of Spiritual Psychology. The mission of the School includes restoring the book as a way of inner transformation and awakening to spirit. We recognize that secondary thought and the reduction of books to sources of information and entertainment as the dominant meaning of reading places in jeopardy the unique character of writing as a vessel of the human spirit. We feel that the continuing emphasis of such a narrowing of what books are intended to be needs to be balanced by writing, editing, and publishing that emphasizes the act of reading as entering into a magical, even miraculous spiritual realm that stimulates the imagination and makes possible discerning reality from illusion in the world. The editorial board of Goldenstone Press is committed to fostering authors with the capacity of creative spiritual imagination who write in forms that bring readers into deep engagement with an inner transformative process rather than being spectators to someone's speculations. A complete catalogue of all our books may be found at www.goldenstonepress.com. The web page for the School of Spiritual Psychology is www.spiritualschool.org.

For Kenny ~

It was everything, it was not nearly enough

TABLE OF CONTENTS

LIGHT WAS EVERYWHERE

WE ARE SAILORS

We are sailors
on a strange dark sea,
shoving our boarded boats
from shore and sand
into riotous nights
of wind and crashing
thunder.

When all sane men
(could we but be)
at home well covered
in dry warm
beds lie lee.

But here our drivenness
and our call,
all soaked and thrown and tossed—
tumbling,
brothered by fear,
lamped by longing—

Find we are

Rowing,
rowing fiercely
towards the darkest center
of the storm.

ATTRACTION

Who would have thought
we would make it so far—
we who have failed
at everything?

So many things
pulled us like magnets,
yet something was stronger
than attraction.
Everywhere we went,
though we tried otherwise,
this was where
we returned.

Being here—
this was being
home.

MOMENT OF SURRENDER

Now.
It's always now,
when the only possibility arises,
and whatever it is you don't want
presents itself:
the cringing ring of the phone,
the dark visitor at the door,
the irritation of your keys
locked against you
inside the house—
whatever the face
or the flavor
or the presence
of what you push away,
you can be sure of this:
your old familiar pain will begin again,
if you cannot pause
as you reach for your gun,
your old and angry words,
the hammer and rusty nails you use
to bar the door,
and remember:
this is the moment
of surrender.

A NIGHT TRAIN PASSES PACIFIC, MISSOURI

Somewhere in the night she wakes,
remembering the flames, the screams,
the rush and tumbled panic. Dimly,
   her dead sister.

Those wet winter days:
nothing would burn in those cheap
tin stoves from Woolworth's.
Cold in the bones and kerosene——or was it
the evil cousin? Once scratched
   a tiny match
      runs everywhere.

Under the covers she remembers:
a blackened mattress on the weedy hill,
the wheeling hawk low overhead,
a huddle on the gravel road,
   nearby a blanket thrown
      over.

Crazy hippies on the hilltop——
four inches ran below the fold.
Forty years later you can buy jeans and
fancy shoes up there;
   stores lined in bright-lit blacktop.

She rolls, she stirs, she dreams again.
The whistle blows and sleepers grind
against the rails.

Under the asphalt,
    old sins lie
        buried.

SERVANT

This one has
held it all together for you—
he's worked so hard,
indeed into a frenzy;
his manic activity and
strange paranoid devices
convinced you he was quite insane—
a total maniac without a license,
driving a ten-ton truck.
Careening around corners and bouncing off walls,
he's built fortresses and castles,
made war with all your neighbors,
and filled the rooms with treasure,
food and beautiful women.
But in the end
he's done it all for you.
Left alone in an empty house,
what could he do
but build a cargo cult
in your own honor?
Now it has become a subdivision,
a city-state of personhood,
built all the way to your front door.
In his last bit of craziness,

he's lowered the drawbridge,
and though he doesn't
know it yet himself, he waits
expectantly, excitedly
for your great,
triumphant
return.

Carried home from battle, after three days the Prince returned to consciousness.

Healed of his wounds, he arose refreshed and called to his physicians and ministers: "Where is my faithful servant, who carried me here at great risk to himself?"

And they answered, "Lord, amazements occurred. You were carried to the gates in the arms of one who appeared just as you do now. When he saw that you were well received, he gave praise to the gods—as though some long and unbearable labor had been finished—and then vanished before our very eyes."

The Prince sent courtiers thoughout the land, searching for this mysterious twin. After many days all reported such a man was nowhere to be found, nor known to exist.

Thereupon the prince—now King—caused a statue to be placed in the town square, carved in his own exact likeness. Beneath it was placed a plaque, upon which were engraved these words:

"To He Who Never Was, who at the cost of his life, saved my Own."

JOURNEY

For years
I thought God
would show up
in a flash and dazzle—
decking me out
in gold and silks,
gifting me with palaces and jewels,
where I would live out
a kingly life of ease.
But these days,
though God looms large
on my horizon—
it is often misty and hard to see.
Our movement
towards each other
comes tightly measured—
in single steps,
in difficult and long lived days.
And our final greeting
may be less
a joyous celebration
full of gold and glitter—
than each,
falling exhausted,
into the others
arms.

LABYRINTH

I must apologize,
for wanting to make things clear,
for connecting A to B to C,
as though there were a line
we could follow, taking us out of
the darkness

a string unwound on the way in,
so that after the slaying was done,
we had a chance to return
where we started

but that was my error,
of wanting a way back, when I
should have known all along—
that being lost and alone in the dark,
was really the only
way out.

ROUGH-HEWN BLOCK

Old friend, you are
a stone pestle ground
by the holy one.
When He began, you were a
rough-hewn block—all
sharpness and edges.
For years he ground you
in the stone bowl of the earth—
sometimes with bones and feathers,
sometimes with iron and steel.
Now you have this
comfortable feeling, sensing
this smoothness that feels
like the thighs of
a woman.
Now is not the time to relax;
all this grinding was
to make of you the
perfect tool:
when you are finished—
that is when
the Real Work
will begin.

BEFORE DAWN

Rocks in a tin can—
the rattle drives you crazy:
words from the books you read,
numbing shows from the TV,
the food you buy,
the clothes you wear,
your mantras meant to keep you
safe from harm;
the money you do or don't make,
the jobs you do all day—
even your dreams at night,
wandering lost in a jumble of worlds.
Rocks everywhere,
banging like crazy,
and worst of all—
no You to be found
anywhere.

A FILE IN MY LOAF OF BREAD

I've lived too long
in this city of right and wrong.
Every friend I knew here
has been imprisoned, tortured
or cruelly put to death.
The jailer's reasons all made perfect sense:
no one could argue with their proofs
or with the truth of what they said.
It's just what's left
is that all my friends are dead.
And so—though it makes no earthly sense—
I must leave this home
where I grew up.
By killing all I loved,
they cut the chains that held me here.
And now the Crazy One—
with his wide bright eyes—
waits for me
outside the gate of the southern wall.
He's cut the bars
and freed the stones around them;
Everything I need is packed,
safe inside my heart.
Tonight on the full moon
two lunatics will flee—
away to the lush, ripe oasis of Zanzibar—
far from this vast grey crumbling city,
the City of the Sane.

OFFERING

The morning is cool
and October;
the two days of rain
have washed us clean,
and the waves
with their crisp white edges
follow the wind
to shore.

The leaves, just beginning
to gold, to yellow,
let light shine through tiny moving
windows. Overhead,
crows wheel
and caw.

I have done all I can do—
which is to say I've
opened a door.

Bowing down,
offering up,
sweeping the temple floor,
lighting the incense.

Even my old self,
that I can find no way to be rid of,
I offer to You,
as I sit amidst the trees
that carry me,
on the wind,
to Beauty.

CRAZY FRIENDS

This morning,
reading the poems
of Han-shan and Shih-te
I feel instantly at peace.
As though my mother
were holding me, whispering
"Shhhsh, don't cry. Everything's all right."
Why does this news from Cold Mountain
calm everything down?
This life is a total mystery
to me, and I find my
face wet with tears.

DEAD MEN

There are two on my bookshelf
who can always save me
when confusion and doubt
drag my soul into a dark
and hopeless pit.

They send a sound of tiny golden bells,
or the scent of fresh baked bread.
How is it these eight-hundred
year old scoundrels can see
me searching,

a blind man stumbling all around
the house—feeling my way toward
their real food, their tender lips
upon my heart?

How is it their love
flows out of everything?
And they—their dead bodies
dust for eons, dance before me
wild and radiant, flooding the room—
the whole world—with life,
and calling me

and dead men everywhere,
to dance!

THE WELL

For most of his life
he carried his most precious gift
hidden, guarded and protected:
the Water of Life—
golden, radiant, glowing, and warm;
held in a crystal heart,
brilliantly transparent,
hung from a chain of woven rubies,
unseen inside the plainness of his robe
and clasped behind his neck.
So that night
when something called him—
when he stumbled in the dark,
led by the sound of rivulet and warble,
out into the vast and treeless desert
under the blazing gemfield
of the black night sky—
Who can tell
what brokenness was opened,
what frozenness flowed away
when in his laughter and his tears,
he holds in the morning light
that Crystal Heart unstoppered;
holds it filling overflowing,
filling once again,
in the bubbling stream
that surges up unending

from the ringed rocks,
golden in the morning sun,
that rim the brightness flowing
from the well.

HOMECOMING

The blue bark rippled
as the waves upon a shore,
the wind, a brush, pushed
upon us with the softness of a lover,
the grass climbed up
the knobby knees that sunk below
the waving green,
while above the gray encircling clouds,
a hush was born that light broke through—
a bird winged by a foot above the ground,
a plane declared a whine upon
the upper air,
and from two hundred feet away,
all violet condensed in irises
of radiant hue,
as rest—a thing I thought that
I could steal to find relief,
came upon me as a gift,
a warmth, a blanket wrapped by
one who loved, around,
to kiss the weariness of
thirty years goodbye, and welcome in
the ancient traveler home.

TRYING TO TELL THE TRUTH

If I said
this was all true,
that would be a lie.
It would be—
at best—a try.
That's what it is,
honest.

I was never good at math,
but my sense of
balance beamed.
It was like a light—
a gift—and
when it rayed, well,
this equaled that,

the way my hand here,
on your breast beats the same—
feel it?—

as your hand,
here,
on mine.

THE RIPPLING OF LIGHT

Perhaps it is your
distress I feel, from
so many miles away—
the effort required to leave,
the effort required to stay.

So often the body, the soul,
seem to pull in different directions—

The body, old and worn,
wants to run again in the sun,
to pick flowers
in the field.

And the spirit swims
in the body—as an ocean—
now heading for the surface,
for the rippling
of light.

Who can say what this struggle is—
to be in the body, alone,
or to leave aloneness
and flow into
everything?

Oh Beauty! Have I left
you behind, when I was young

and blessed as the flowers
and the summer day?

Or do you flow now,
towards me as you always do,
from the deep mystery
of our one beloved Heart?

Once, everything was distinct,
and each thing had
its own place
in the world.

Now the edges are removed,
and blessedly, I am
inside of everything.

This morning, though bitter cold,
the sun rose brightly and birds flew
overhead.

And I, praising everything
that is or will be,
flew with them.

WHERE HAVE I GONE?

You thought I went away,
off into the blackness
of non-existence,
while you were left alone,
abandoned again.
Yet who was I—
other than this one inside you,
the one who now longs for me
with an aching heart?
Was I really someone
outside you—
Someone other than this
loneliness you now feel?
Someone other than this sunrise
that fills your heart
with brightness,
the same way we once filled
each others?
Tell me, as you touch
your Love within you—
where have I gone?
I did not go away—
I came in.

A POEM THAT ALMOST WASN'T

Here is a life
that almost wasn't.
The odds, really,
were all against it.
But I remembered,
I was *re-minded*:
You only get one chance,
over and over again,
until you don't.

Then all chances
are gone, used up.

So breathe
your precious life
into whatever you love—
let it really be there,
for once,
Alive.

It's the only chance
any of us will
ever get.

DAY AFTER DAY

Every day
the dice are thrown.
Rumi says,
"Read what has been
given you."
This day tumbled
out of the master's hand,
and every one
of those days has
been a gift.
Don't be distressed
by thoughts of
winning and losing—
think of the One
who rolls,
and how you come
each day out
of darkness—
anxious, yet trusting
the light will be
there.
What is rolled,
is rolled.
It's His face,
his hands,
you came to see.

THE NIGHT PRAYER

Full of fear in the night,
I asked God for strength—
He said, "You have always
been fearless!"

Feeling so empty and alone
I asked God to fill me—
He said, "You have always
been Full."

Feeling so separate and adrift,
I asked God to hold me—
He said, "Dear one, since time began,
you have never been out
of my arms."

And so, in peace at last,
I slept.

RUNNING OUT OF TIME

The thought was,
I could apologize,
I could ask for your forgiveness—
    but why?

For wanting to let you know,
as the years lurch forward again,
cogs in the cosmic wheel,
grinding ignorance to dust,

    that somehow I have been blessed,
to travel these roads with you;
that I would give anything,
to take away your pains,

    to travel these roads again,
only this time, with more love,
this time, most of all,
with kindness.

FIRST BLACKBERRIES

You know the feeling:
the cool freshness of
an early summer day,
light lying all around you,
doing its slow dance with shadows—
you, floating in your chair
or hammock,
inside the song of birds,
the chatter of squirrels and chipmunks,
rocking while standing still,
held by the whole thing—
you, sucked dry of yourself,
moistened, christened,
rewet with dew and the
vibration of this day,
like a slow wind gathering,
the way those big white clouds do—
piling, building—into
something immense,
something unimaginable.

CATERPILLAR

Caterpillar,
stub-legged wonder!
Nature's couch potato,
munching all day on the couch
itself.
While the sun is bright and
the leaves are fat—
what thought could there
be of anything else?

Then the mysterious call:
no one hangs back—
"Not me! I've got more
leaves to eat!"

Maybe it's a certain
dry taste in the mouth.
Maybe one more bite would
split you wide open.
But something starts the silk
to spinning.

Round and round yourself
it goes: the warm white room
growing about you—a softness
built of summer days,
green leaves and blue sky.

When you shut your pillowed door,
what happens is hidden
from us all.

For days and nights of sun,
rain, wind and moon
your white boat rocks
over the sea.

We know what happens next.
Is that You, green one,
raising your wet head and spiraled mouth
into the World?

Who are you now?
Amazed, we watch as you
unfurl in majesty.
Now high above the wind
you gaze below:

Everywhere, bright stars
explode in the vast
green air.

SOON

Bud of life,
let go of what
you might become—
pictures in your mind
of other flowers
blooming.
Feel your own sap,
the green electric
tingle of cells climbing
your stem,
building around you
yellow and gold
translucence.
Let yourself be pushed
by your own Self—
up, out and free
into Spring's cold blue air—
warmed by the
brilliant light everywhere.
Then let them in,
those clear-winged
buzzing beings,
to wander in your golden
soul-dust—
offer it freely to
their gathering arms—

let them mix
your essence with
the sweetness of a
thousand flowers,
become as you
were meant to be—
honey of love,
Sweet taste of
Joy.

JOURNEYMEN

September's last
morning glory rose,
round and beautiful and blue,
a fluted cup
filling up with light,
drinking deeply in the cold
October air.
Arrayed around
were all the future flowers,
seeds safely in their pods
still green,
soaking in that light as well,
filling up with
flowerness.
So she drank it in—
the last rare ray—
to seal their souls upon
their winter journey,
through cold and snow and ice
to earth's embrace,
to sinking deep and searching out,
the darkness, and at last,
the Light.

HARVEST

Fistfuls of stones
from the path,
grass and leaves drawn
from the moonstone starlitter
along the road,
broken shards of last years'
branches brown and shredded—
gathered here,
tight in your hands.
Squeeze!
Tightly squeeze!
Until the blood runs red
between your fingers,
the autumn harvest,
Life,
grapesweet god
pouring forth, dripping,
a flood from your fingers
and wrists,
a waterfall fills the golden cup,
catching it all—
thick, deep red of a billion hearts,
every drop alive—
and you drink,
God! You drink!
You drink as a stone
broken open discovers
a million years
of thirst.

DERVISH BY NUMBER

Outside my window
the mystery of snow is falling.
This weekend two feet fell,
and I remember my amazement
when I learned that
no two snowflakes are alike—
I imagine myself,
tiny tweezers and magnifying glass,
checking each flake carefully,
stacking fragile crystals
into piles to fill a cup of glistening
refractions,—rainbows
and dry ice—
friendly emissaries from the angels
and the stars.
How many lie within one inch?
Or in a cubic foot?
Or in the hundred-thousand feet
that cover my back yard?
Who could count them all?
Even wild-eyed Dr. Einstein
or the stellar Mr. Hawking
must defer to these
millions of white angels,
who gaze so quietly
from the head of their pin.

So I let my mind go.
I set it free
to bounce and skip and reel.
Joining hands I dance,
swinging my partner—who smiles
at me all
lace and diamond—
until blown and drifted and whirling
I fall in white exhaustion,
feeling the soft white closeness
as each curtsied partner
billows down about me,
as my breathing
slows and quiets—
and we,
the uncountable,
stare up to watch
the Moon.

ROSE INTO VIOLET

The frost on the roof top
glows from the morning darkness—
rose light filling up
the cup of the world.

I remember days of long ago,
shivering outside with frozen hands,
carrying water in a bucket
from a well.

Frost crunching under foot,
bird calls clear against a leafless sky,
cold air sharp as glass in my chest—

shrinking from the chill,
yet something flowing out
and in at the same time.

The rose light shifts to violet,
and I am full of the bite of Life—
the bitter, sweet fragrance
of the Real.

DIMLY

Wings—emerge
from my own body!
I cannot tell
if I am caught in a
cocoon gone wrong
and stillborn—
or in the
timeless hours between
the weaving of the skein
and the slow pulse
of Spring.
Fear of not emerging
is no help—
but this new body
strains so mightily
for birth,
for the full light
of day!

SPRING

From the doorway of the window
we regarded each the other:
I the world, and the wide world, me.

And as I felt my self flow out,
into the wonder of each created thing,
the leaf, the tree, the sky,
the stones upon the ground—

So the world flowed in,
to marvel at the universe of feeling:
the sadness, grief, the happiness, the simple joy
of childhood, the warmth and love
that filled the open heart.

We became the inbreath and the outbreath:
the world outside brought deep within the heart,
the feeling of the heart filled all the former
outside world of things.

We were lovers closer than the closest lovers.

So we watched until we turned away,
yet now the world came in where
only I had been before—
and into open arms, I so long inside,
stepped out.

YOU

Every day you wake up
and here you are—
you again!

Something keeps bringing you back,
over and over again.

For so many years,
with so much dedication—
through years of tiny bodies,
strong green shoots of boyhood,
fumbling fatherhood, and now
grey-haired, grandfathered.

Who has been so faithful
to carry you all this way?

Who could see so much in you,
to invest so much time?

Turning off the stove,
looking quietly past the tired eyes
in the mirror,

who is watching?
Who is looking at you now
with so much interest,
with so much love?

RESCUED

(AS IN THE RELIEF OF BEING FOUND)

Tonight, hurled
exhausted into the world,
I find that I am saved.

Saved by the Earth, herself.

The sky, the trees,
the high thin clouds, all come to my rescue—
all give themselves without asking.
And I feel, *this is the way it is*—
unlimited blessing:

Bodies breaking like bubbles,
we are rolled in a tide
of Beauty.

In oceans of pearls and rubies,
rounded on shores of diamonds and gold—
age after age of Beings are born—
loving and lost
but not losing,
the beauty over always.

And the ocean is full and moving—
Always more are rolled to the shore, to love.
Always more, are rolled again, to love us.

And the foam
sparkles in our hands,
dripping diamonds and fire
as the sun sets and the universe turns,
and the Earth gives,
and gives,
and gives
forever.

THIS WORLD

The silent realm,
the formless realm,
the realm of vast and undistinguished Void.
Realm of sinking into,
realm of letting go,
featureless land of great relief.
Realm of no particular
particularity.
Oh, such blessed relief!
But sitting outside in October,
with the distant insect people
droning their soft, sonorous chants—
And the wind rippling and uplifting
leathery leaves full of their own
pattering songs—
And the complexity,
the multiplicity of twigs,
and curling leaves, and orange pine needles fallen,
and all the twisting, colliding
patterns in the bark—
And the crossing branches opening
patterned doorways of light to the
beings of the grey-white sky—
All these call to me as they dance
and move, floating on the same air
that flows about my face.
All these call in some way

that the silent realm leaves silent and
unspoken, as it must—
And I want more than anything to
hold them both,
like a wife and a lover, both in the same bed.
But only beauty herself beheld
calls out from me, if the choice is given:
This World! This World!
This World!

GEORGIA O'KEEFFE IN BUFFALO

Focused on the rust red strokes
of bone bleached arroyos,
eroding under blue blazed brightness,
immense and silent
I did not see her standing,
gazing with great intensity past my shoulder;
or notice her presence shadowing mine,
as I moved from frame to frame,
expecting here and there some lesser work
to prove these all were studies;
exercises that exposed some hesitance or fear,
some mortality of smallness.

Instead, presuming a
pastoral symphony of light,
I wandered lulled by soft grey hills
and blue green pastel sage,
and so was taken unawares
by her soft but steely grip upon my shoulder,
steering me from one painting
to the next.

Sunlight and alkali poured out upon me,
more upon more,
until thunder I did not know
arisen broke about me,
and I cried aloud—

For the gods had gathered
and grabbed me from behind,
their arms all full of strength
and rippling muscle.

Guardians of Art
shifted their nervous eyes, uncertain.
Hands fluttered above unholstered
walkie-talkies.
But the rain had moved on,
past the distant pinioned hills of Ghost Ranch,
as we did, around and through what
others thought were rooms,
but we knew were

the temple of a woman
who had wrestled long with God,
until they both cried out
and then became
The World.

MONDAY MORNING

Did I ever tell you
how great you are?

Did I ever say,
"It's just so wonderful you're here"

Have I ever hugged you
when you thought that you were bad?

Do you know your face
is like the Sun to me?
That when I see you, my whole body
feels warm, and safe and loved?

You know,
in all the world of what you do
and how you do it,
It's—just—fine.

You always do it "right"
even when you think
you did it wrong!

If I said, (and I do say it now)
that you are Joy beyond belief,
you are such Happiness
that I can barely stand it—

that just to be around you
makes me dance, and jump,
unable to be still,

would you believe me?

Go now. Look into the mirror
and tell me what you see:

"Hello my Friend! It's Us in here.
Come out and play away the day with Me."

You think I'm just a voice inside your head,
or a poem written from a friend—
But really I am just your own Love
speaking—shouting out,

"I'm so glad you're here!
So glad that you've come Home!"

BEAUTIFUL WOMEN

Only the beautiful women
can save us
from the end of
this cold frozen winter,

only beautiful women
with their dark eyes
and soft souls
peering out

from fur-lined afghans
and warm sweaters,
with their promise to hold
God's directive—

to welcome us,
the hairy and unkempt,
the worn and oak-kegged,
weather boarded men;

only beautiful women,
no matter what age,
no matter how large or small,
prune wrinkly or slippery smooth,
all of them the only

glorious way we will ever
get to Spring,
to new life, to the place where
our chests beat again

with love,
banging over and over
until our ribs crack and the
light flows out—

only the beautiful women
can do it, with their
strong intent fists,
their sharp white teeth,

their grip like iron,
their incredible,
undefeatable
beauty.

NO NEED TO CALL IT ANYTHING

You always knew it—
those days when you were young—
how the world shone,
and each piece of it
was precious.
Only age and the wrong kind
of instruction stole
it away,
and left you with
paper words instead of
brightness.
But now it's back,
that amazing music that
everything makes:
leaves talking to the wind,
ants climbing a tree in a desert caravan,
the water running from
the brook of a bird.
You always knew it—
there was just no need to
call it anything,
like you might do today,
the way you might say,
God.

BREATH

Sometimes it would all
settle down—
the pain in the legs,
the pictures, the movies of
misshapen demons and naked
women climbing in and out
of each other,
and there was only the breath,
the in and out of it,
going so slowly,
nothing else at all
save for a bird or two,
or the slam of a car door two doors down,
or the whine and grind of a
garbage truck, the banging of cans,
getting farther and farther away—
then nothing, again, at all—
like a lake, like a bed
crisp and clean in the morning,
like the breath going
in and out, so slowly,
nothing else—
then the bell.

EACH OTHER

Who do we have
but each other,
here where everything begins?

The pines stand sentinel
outside the backyard window,
the cat circles your feet
waiting to be fed.

What stands by us is what lives with us—
not what we choose;
what has chosen us instead.

The chipped dishes
in the sink that bring breakfast
every day to your
hungry mouth;

the worn rug
on the steps to the mud-room floor,
that accepts your dirty feet
whenever you enter the house;

the mailbox that opens wide
to receive your hand as it brings
you news of the world
outside.

What have they but you?
You, who polish their painted
bodies and shine their silver wheels,
who clean their serviceable clothes,
who hang them in the
summer air to dance.

Or the long-haired woman who
walks past your driveway
every morning,

the check-out girl
who smiles her secret smile
as you buy a second
bar of chocolate,

the soft black dog
with her deep dark eyes,
who drops her favorite toy
into your lap.

Who do we have but each other?

The partner you took
for this life,
your new love of the moment,

those you little regarded
but worked with for years?

Those who bring pain
or grief and annoyance?
Those whose affection touches
you with love?

Who is left
if we leave out those
who bore witness around us?

They are the messengers
of what matters—

who hold up their yellowed
paper and the penciled
words against the window
of the door between us:

"We,
Us,
Each Other"

❧ INTERLUDE ❧

SONG OF ATTACHMENT

Oh lord,
let me keep this house,
let me keep this job.
Oh lord,
let me not grow old
and die,
nor any of those I like
just the way they are:
my wife, children
and grandchildren.
Let my favorite TV programs
never go off the air,
or at least be available
on DVD.
Lord, let my driveway
never be filled with
snow and ice,
nor my yard filled with
grubs and weeds.
Lord, let no change
come into this house,
unless it be
so that I may lose 30 pounds
and have all of my
diminished sexual
functioning restored.
Lord, let no more
of my hair be lost,

nor more spots appear
upon my skin.
May illness never visit me;
may an unknown
relative or stranger die
and leave me
a million dollars in
their will.
Lord, let gasoline prices
and taxes rise no further—
in fact, it would be
OK if those went down.
Let my car never be
subject to rust or
expensive repair,
and may my tires
always keep a thick
and heavy tread.
Lord, please keep the
universe just the way
I like it, only better.
For this lord, I pray,
in your name,
amen.

WHAT IT COULD BE

It could be a
door slamming,
it could be a bird
singing.

It could be bacon
in the pan
or the weatherman
on TV.

It could be your toe
inside your sock,
it could be the cats scratching
at the door;

it could be your eyes
blinking open,
after a thousand years
of sleep.

SACRIFICE

Every morning,
after rising,
I sit alone and test my blood.

Before the sun awakens,
before my coffee's made
or my eyes have quite adjusted
to another brightening day;

after the cats are fed,
after my books and pills are
carefully arranged—
then comes the click
I prick my finger
with a sharp and shiny needle.

Tiny, quick, the bite remains the same,
as slowly rises round
the bright red drop
above the horizon of my thumb—

And for an instant,
before the numbers test
the sweetness of my blood,

my inside greets my outside
and a bright red stain connects us—

announcing the offering again:
my life in bargain, fairly,
for this beautiful new day.

HALF LIGHT

In the morning darkness
I pull on yesterday's wrinkled
pants and shirt and feel in the dim light
for my glasses and sandals.
Shuffling downstairs I set
the thermostat against the morning chill
and feed the cats on
little paper plates.

As the coffee gurgles
into the pot
I stare out the window over
the kitchen sink.
Squinting,
trees and bushes bloom
from the dark grey violet
blanketing the yard.
A squirrel shivers and
shakes his tail;
a jay swoops and lands
upon the feeder.

In the half light
I stare at my transparent
reflection in the window—

half myself and half
the blue world outside.

Bit by bit the dim world brightens,
as I dissolve completely,
until only the new day
remains.

REMEMBERING THE REAL

How wonderful the first mornings
of summer—those bright days after school
had closed, and waking was to
birds singing and sun rising

There was no place to go or be but there,
where everything was wonder:
rock, wood, bright broken glass—
a gear in the gravel, an unknown bit of metal

wedged between tarred wooden sleepers
and the metal rail.
No more books or papers—all day
was an exploration of weeds and the skeletons
of mice or half built buildings

Tramping for miles, looking for the real,
carrying some cast off bit of boxcar home
to dream on—floating on the wave
of what was, right then,

with nothing longed for,
searching for nothing that wasn't there,
for it all was

RADIO

I remember the long highway miles,
the hours of darkness between the lights of towns,
the whine and rhythmic thump of the large black tires,
as my father drove us from St. Louis to Chicago
in the middle of the night.

I remember the endless black fields
flying by in the warm humid summer wind,
the orange-lit windows of distant farmhouses,
the heavy rumblings of a passing train.

I remember the radio, of how little there was of it,
yet how much it filled, fading in and out of the static,
and then the lush melodies of *Laura, Autumn
Leaves,* or *Deep Purple*.

It was a language of melancholy learned early,
barely heard and always distant,
as we traveled in the darkness that filled the world,
between distant points of light.

Once you called it
everyday reality.
The world of things was
more real than any world
of spirit, because
it was so absolutely,
purely, here.

You said, *"The scientists
are right—this is the only
reality there is."*
Because of the truth of it.
Because your eyes saw
that it was so.

Back then you
really saw the real,
but rarely so.
Once seen, you fell
into the mind. For
years and years you never
knew there was a dark
side of the moon.

Now you see both sides
of form and emptiness.
Presence comes with you

to the table, where you caress
your cup of tea, and savor
the taste of your toast.

Once as a child
you broke open a stone
and marveled as the light
of preciousness—pure
presence of being—
flowed out like the Sun.

Now here you are today,
an old man worrying about
money, your health, about how
and where you will live
in the future.

Yet your heart still yearns
for the stone,
as you, the breakfast table
and the crumbs on your plate
watch the dark window,
waiting in confidence,
for dawn.

SIMPLE THINGS

When you're young
you give it no mind—
anyone, anything, will do.

Only when you're older
do simple things grow
precious:

your black stone cup
with the oval rim, the
porcelain white within—

the smoky plastic pencil
with the rubber grip, the replaceable
eraser, the strong thin lead—

the dark mornings before dawn,
the lifting edge,
the first wide call,

your old friend glowing,
rising toward you,
reaching out his
hand.

ALL TIME FAVORITES

Some days God
decides to play
the oldies:
A brilliant sunrise,
some soft new snow;
birds in the garden,
foxes in the field.
Fresh iced tea and lemonade,
tomatoes on the vine;
tiny leaves in springtime,
a bright full moon.
Falling in love,
waking early on a
summer day—
He could go on forever,
spinning these tunes
he loves so well:
now he's dancing to the music,
headphones held tight
upon his head—
sending this one out to
Donny from
Denise way down
in Georgia:
Don't forget July
she says—
love's old sweet
song.

PICTURE THIS

Looking back
into the old photograph,
to who you were twenty years ago,
your mind says: *"I was so much happier then,
and so much younger."*
But were you?
Back there—in that picture place—
you looked forward
toward this time,
didn't you?

There, you held your own invisible picture,
you saw yourself in this future life:
more at peace, happier, wealthier for sure,
all your problems solved.
It was a dream, wasn't it?

So imagine a picture of now,
in a frame on your bedside when you are old,
taking your last breath.
Look at the way you were—
the way you are now—
from then.
Smile for the camera.
Make it a love letter
to yourself.

THE SNOW, THE STONES, THE LIGHT

The window held the frame
of all outdoors

I watched the single flakes of snow
float down

they fell so slow—I watched them close
and to a quarter mile away

I could have walked between them
with a smile

and on the window ledge sat
seven stones arrayed

receiving on their roundedness
the upper edge of light

and where I looked for revelation
once before, the presence of

the stones, the light, the snow
was everything, was more.

YOU'VE SEEN IT

You've seen it, I know.
Maybe in your wife,
as she bounces your grand-daughter
on her knee.
Or in your old friend,
grey-haired at the podium,
talking about her
new book.
Something gets in
past the gears of the mind—
a laugh, an unforeseen
sweetness.
And it happens.
The old face falls away—
and in a shiver of
transparency,
the young one, ageless,
glows before you like a god—
brighter, more real
than the way She and You
always were.
Then the light fades
and the old wrinkled face
comes back.

But newer now.
Flowing upward from
the heart—
You can still catch it:
See, there it is.
In the
eyes.

THIRTEEN

I remember you—
the long December walks
in tall dry grass and weeds
along the railroad tracks;
the abandoned spikes,
iron cold and rusty
in the winter sun;
the bone-white skull
abandoned by the barbed-link fence,
fine-boned mummy fur
a tapestry of wonder
in a blessed body.
You were there—
crunching underfoot
among the stones and broken
glass between the ties;
in the thistle's spiny husk—
the drift of milkweed,
in the faceted red
depth of a broken piece
of plastic.
You held me in your fierce kiss—
that white hot wind
burning into me,
fur pulled tight around
my ears—there as we walked,

as we examined the nooks
and crannies of the world,
as I fell away from
who I never was anyway—
and it was only us,
we without a name,
gloriously alive.

BELOVED

If I sent a love song
it would be a mirror,
reflecting your own face,
the one you push away.

But you would see instead,
My face and be astounded,
for this mirror would be magic
and allow your heart to see,

that what you thought, for all those years,
was something less than worthy,
was Beauty, full and present,
transcendent in Her glory,

for the face you see
that once was you,
now you see is Me.

RECOGNITION

I watched you next to me—
someone not yet known—
yet found within your face,
your hands, the perfect movement of your body,
the companion of a thousand years.
Recognition shimmered—
that breeze upon the lake—
and there you were: unknown in fifty years
of worldly ways, as clear sunlight
through an open window.
Brother, sister, lover—we traveled
on a journey linked through endless lifetimes,
filled with joy, with love,
with seeming separation—
yet here we were set side by side,
eyes lit up by seeing over centuries:
we who searched so far away,
found by coming home.

LOOK FOR NO OTHER LOVER

This morning's breeze,
after days of burning silence, says:

Look for no other lover.

I am the true one
who greets you each morning;
I wrap the world about your shoulders,
I kiss you with what is.

Do not forget,
as you often do,
that there is no holy place
more holy than here,
in my Presence.

For so long
you have seen me,
and thought I was just the world,
or someone you knew,
or any ordinary thing.

I arrived here before you,
waiting to offer you
everything—

See now,
with your heart's
new opened eyes—
the ones that look at all things,
and this day

see Me everywhere.

KRISPY-KREME BODHISATTVA

Last night I told Vicki:
"I want to become a wandering monk—
A Krispy-Kreme monk",
I said.

I'd wander homeless,
with no more worries,
and beg donuts from the shop
on Jefferson Road.

To people coming out I'd say:
"I'll give you sweetness too"
and in trade I'd give a hug, a smile.
I'd say: "How beautiful you are!"

Then, filled with sweetness,
we'd share a Krispy-Kreme together.

At night the manager would come
and shake his broom at me:
"Go home, old monk.
Stop bothering my customers."

I'd hug him too and say,
"You're right. It's late. I'm on my way."

Then off I'd go,
into the fields beyond the highway.

I'd sit beneath dark trees and watch
the evening sky grow bright.

"Hey Moon," I'd say,
before I fell asleep.
"Here's one last donut—I saved it
just for You."

LOVE FOR SALE

I have become
a merchant of Love,
selling piecemeal from
the trunk of my car.
Hundreds pass me by each day,
so afraid of my ragged joy.
But for those who risk
my wild-eyed strangeness,
I have a bargain
they could never guess:
their stopping *was* my payment,
and in return
I fill their hands
with Rubies and with Emeralds,
Sapphires dripping
like blue fire—
"Enough!" they cry,
yet still I pour
the Jewels of my Heart—falling
through their fingers,
gathering like
Spring's blossoms,
drifted
around their feet.

THE LIGHTNESS OF TOUCH

It was all about
gentleness, the
lightness of a touch

How we started from a dream,
one we can't remember
except for the fear,
the racing heart

And we turned to the one beside us,
and maybe it was our
own arms

We touched lightly and
with gentleness—
we knew it was all love,
that nothing anywhere

was wrong

WHOSE NAME I CANNOT SAY

So will you join with me
and say I see it too
that light that shines from your
and all those other faces

and say it is an oath
that I will never let it die
I will love it 'til the end of time and on beyond

this light of which I do not know the meaning
but shakes me trembling like a tender
bright green leaf

that says in some great way
that this is me and this is you
and what my heart would die
would live for
and that it is not mine

or yours but yes it is
and all of it is you whose name
I cannot say
except as

ANYTHING

The stranger said, "Look, you really have little time. One day or twenty years, it's all the same. You've spent your previous time, your whole life so far, serving those you thought of as your masters. As though their approval, their point of view, was more real, more important than your own. You blamed it on ego, when really Ego blamed it on you.

So the time has come, just as it has each day, to go your own way. Not out of selfishness, but just because you'll never get another chance. Claim what you've always claimed but were afraid to— because, you said, of others. This is your doorway of opportunity. Step through it now, while you can."

At this the stranger vanished, and the sky, though cloudy, was clear, and I felt all around me a silence, and a voice that said, *"Anything"*.

SATURATION POINT

The pieces have been here
all your life.
Moved around the table,
sliding back and forth,
some fitting,
some impossible.
You stare and study
until your eyes blur
and your head aches.
You know each piece so well.
You've studied them so long.
Until the day comes
when it's all finally enough:
the last drop is added,
or something that was forever
hard and pointed
is smoothly worn away.
From everywhere, at once,
the crystal grows its patterns:
the lace and link
of all those puzzle parts
is perfectly remade,
and last night's pain
and tomorrow's joy
find each other at last.

Like brothers and
sisters,
like lovers,
like the Sun rising
on the day you,
and everyone else,
were born.

REMEMBRANCE

During the day
I say I'll remember—
but then of course,
once again,
I forget.
Sitting down,
getting quiet,
once again—it's just
Me and You.
In the old days,
the church on the hill
rang out the
quarter-hour.
Nowadays it is
our job
to swing the striker,
to make each thing
we do
ring like a bell.

PRAYER

Every day
I ask for miracles,
and each day
greets me in its ordinary way,
with sun shine and bird song,
gray clouds and rain.

Each day I pray for
the beautiful and the ecstatic,
and once again I am
greeted by your smiling face of forty years,
and the bright lit bread crumbs
on my plate after breakfast.

Each time I ask for more,
you give me the same old things,
and here am I,
an old man down on his knees,
head bent low to the ground.

It may look like prayer,
but I am only searching for gold
in the grass,
and always finding
You.

MIDAS

What a simple secret!
Like Midas,
every touch is gold!
But here,
the gold is Life!
And every
place you light upon
explodes—
blossoms burst
from dead dry wood—
each touch,
the treasure of your
One True Love,
touching back
at you.

MORE GOLDEN

What gold could be more golden
than the ground I see around me,
than the dried leaves laid precisely,
than the quiet movement of the pines
before the storm?
"I was a hidden treasure,"
that secret song that sang me,
that never was a traitor though I
sometimes thought it so.
For hidden does mean hidden,
and treasure is the gift we all received,
received by opening up our eyes—
the ones that we were given—
that came along with heart, that
brought as well the body,
no, nothing comes alone, and
every hiding brings a finding,
that we were never watchers,
who saw the gold outside us,
but were instead bright gold itself
reflected in Your eyes.

DISGUISE

All day long
we play our frightful games
in the wilderness, as spies,
sea captain or peg-legged pirate,
spitfire ace or
French collaborateur.
Home at night
we are unmasked,
hanging up our costumes,
throwing down our bodies
into deep cushioned chairs before the fire,
brandy in hand,
laughing to ourselves—
at first a smile, a chuckle,
then gut-wrenching roars
until we cry
with grief—
amazed at how skillfully
we played the game,
at how utterly and completely
we fooled ourselves
so well.

I HAVE NOT LOST

So it seems to slip away,
and in my sadness close my eyes—

whereupon the breeze
comes forth,
the birds around me sing
inside the trees,
the morning sun falls upon and
brightens my left eye,

and I know again
in great relief,
I have not lost but gained,
for *I am this,*
wherein all does arise;

and once again relax
my mad deluded dance, that
tried to make the world go round
within the midst of chaos.

INFINITY

On days when I forget,
I travel morning to evening
in search of you—
my most precious love, lost.
Without rest,
I frantically look here and there,
anxiety rising and feeling
empty inside.
Other days, I remember:
here you are in everything I see and touch.
We are so close there is no difference
between us.
All day long we caress each other,
laughing at everything,
falling asleep in each other's arms.
Moon rising, sun setting—
forgetting where you are, all I want
is to remember;
remembering,
all I want is to never
forget.

LATTICE

We are so intimate
with the World…
breathing brings her in…
exhaling, she flows out.

The eye closes,
and we float in inner space—
the eye opens,
and we no longer have edges,

but are filled with mountains
and flowers, thunderstorms
and fireflies.

And the ear opens clear
day and night—
birdsong and windstorm,
hammer and tong.

Our body is but a breezeway—
bells ringing,
stars shining,
inside and out.

THINGS I CAN COUNT ON

I don't know how it will work,
but what does that matter?
My heart, my lungs, my blood—
they do what they do on their own—
and I go along for the ride.

Oh the time will come when they skip a beat,
and worry will set in. As though I could
reset the thermostat, or adjust
a screw here or there.

But things will work in their own way,
with gifts I can always count on—
like sunrise and rain and snow,
like love in the springtime,
like death, and a smile.

Oh yes, that smile....

WIDE OPEN WINDOW

Sitting this morning
with the full moon,
unable to sleep—

the moon moving slowly
past the locust's budding branches.
Humid but clear
out the open window,

spring peepers at three a.m.,
starting and stopping—
and my mind,

free from fear,
so unexpectedly empty
and at peace.

YOU AND I

We belong together,
you and I.
What we bring to each other
turns both of us precious—an elixir
indescribably sweet.

Like cream for my coffee,
like sugar and salt,
our combination improves
everything we touch.

Once I thought, within my isolation,
that it was all You.
Now it is you—living inside
my heart—that has created gold and light
for the both of us.

On that day I know, you allowed
me in as well.

This talk seems to be about
inside and outside,
but really it's about how each of us—
so long alone—find we have
always been together,

here where we always were,
here where we always
belonged.

RADIANCE

Past yourself
I see,
radiance illumined—
Who You Are,
and forever in infinity
will be;
and overwhelmed,
my heart bows down
before your shining majesty,
as you upon your
knees are lit
by that great light
that radiates
from Me.

THE VOICES

Today I could tell
the voices
were tired.
They, like I, had been
down this road
so many times.
It was old work and
all of us felt
the exhaustion,
how we'd given it our all,
a long time ago,
and more.
We simply sat and looked
at each other,
I with my new face
that had grown old,
they with their sepia tones
and slightly rippled edges.
We both knew it was time
to go, and I felt their
happiness rise with
my own.
The breeze had come up,
and they thinned
like high clouds
reaching for the deeper sky,
for the brighter light.

The wonder! they sighed
in dissolving,
such joy and relief
in letting go,
in coming home,
in saying—at last—
goodbye.

A BOOK WITH GOLDEN EDGES

So the day came
when I slid down into the sea
of my own desire—
where I remembered the joy
of my best friends on a summer day
of no responsibility, except to my own Joy
in the discovery of things,
where an oily threaded bolt or
a fresh drilled hole in a rough pine board
was as exciting and new as the ripening
peach above me on the tree,
or the whirling snail under the cool
dripping faucet on the backyard brick.
There I loved myself with
no thought of myself—
only the freedom of being, and the
amazement under every rock and stone,
or the million year interior when
the rock split open—in the channeled canals
on a broad green leaf, in the ecstasies of water,
sun and the whole world open like
a book with golden edges,
where each page turned was newer
than the last. And so today
I found my way back, out of the cellar room
where I had locked myself:

And it was all there!

The same sun shone with its radiant heat,
the sky wore her original blaze of blueness,
all my friends—
their faces newly changed
to yours, and yours, and mine—
came rushing, running in that
pell-mell sneaker slap of Summer,
into the arms of being alive,
here in the heat of the heart of the world,
into the dizzy, whirling embrace
of the freedom of our own
Desire!

THERE IS NO END

There is no end to your
coming and going, no end to the praise
and sorrowing I bring to the
wonder of your name.

Already the cicada
senses autumn, dry leaves appear
scattered on the grass.
The garden bears the scars
and bruises that we who all have
aged, now bear.

But fruit tumbles out in profusion,
as though to say—Yes, I am bent and old,
half a cripple—yet still I give,
more than you can possibly imagine,
by the magic, by the gift,
of this love.

HEART WORK

In the end, like a gift,
joy is given.
One battles to step through
the fear, the ignorance and pain—
the worst inflicted early and your own—
and finds, on the other side of grief,
a hand held out to help you up,
to draw you close and hold you,
to ache along with you in heart's
great grief-racked wounding—
then wipe away the tears and stare
into each other's eyes,
so deep that depth now has no name;
to find upon your lips the
widening of a smile,
to feel it grow beyond what bodies
can contain: breaks out, explodes in
freedom's cry of sobbing joy—
all life, which is no longer
yours alone, but which,
in Great Totality,
you claim.

ANGEL

Inwardly she rises,
the one you always wanted:
protector, warrior, fierce queen
of the bright blade.
She confers no invulnerability
to the body, but builds
your inner bones of steel.
Bodies are cut down,
wounds suffered, and age abets decay.
Her strength, you will see in time,
was all your own: Inviolability.
The One you both guard
needs no protection:
you and she are essential parts.
Body blunts the blow that
aims to damage spirit;
She comes—not only inner strength—
but Strength Herself.
Past her no foe can find an entry:
all weapons lose their power,
and Who We Are moves forward
into silence, able now through her,
to serve.

RIPE

You are a particular
kind of fruit—
no other is so sweet.

I have gardened long—
in the garden of all gardens—
pruning your vines and tendrils,
shaping your errant leaves.

I have given you my full face of Light,
every day of your being—
and in the evenings, the absolute
love of the moon.

You have been bitten, cut, buffeted by storms.
Insects and elements have attacked you,
but I am far the stronger;

now you are luscious, delicious,
the fruit of our mutual hours of labor.
Your sweetness is almost complete—

when you will shine, held in our hand—
nourishing the world with fulfillment,
with the ecstasy of your
own taste.

I do not think there
will be grief,
I think there will be joy,
when we recognize
each other
and can only see the best;
that our sorrows
and our failings will have
dropped like
leaves in Autumn,
and we—now bare and clear and
brilliant to each other—
stand radiant with love,
with praise and joy
for who we are,
joined together as we
always were,
golden pillars
at the end of time.

FALLING ASLEEP IN LATE AFTERNOON

I wake.
And for an instant
there is no memory,
no time,
and I am falling through
morning or afternoon,
to or from evening or day,
past seasons of no reckoning—
grabbing at names,
faces, places, times
until one sticks like a rope
and I jerk,
floating feet first toward
something I remember,
out of freedom,
and back into
the world.

My fear
and my joy
are doing this
amazing dance—
Fear wants
to flee—joy grabs her hand
and swings her
around:
"See!" joy cries,
"The more we whirl and spin,
the more we turn into
something new!"
Fear jumps in—
"Oh, I'm so good at running
fast," she says.
Now they whirl together,
like atom and
electron—
Look!
It's magic!
Light is pouring out!

THE SWEETNESS

It is all breaking in
around me,
the sweetness, the bliss,
the unfounded hope;
everywhere light is pressing
at the windows,
tenderness is crowding,
kindness is streaming through keyholes,
beauty is overfilling
the darkness,
leaving no room for despair,
for the old cruelties,
the tiny cuts,
the red wounds and the blood.
I asked, I prayed,
and had hoped to find pennies.
I could never conceive,
though I used the words,
that Light was
everywhere.

THE JEWEL

It is morning again, dark and early.
We are one week away
from winter.
Outside the window I can see no light,
only the reflections of the kitchen counter,
last night's dishes stacked
in the sink.
I feel myself wandering the old pathways again,
the ones with empty rooms where
I search for the jewel, for
the stairs to the cave of Aladdin.
Through the window I can almost see the trees,
black against the field.
The wind blows—its sound
is clear to my ear.
I turn off the kitchen light and
stand in the darkness.
Outside, the real world
leaps into brightness.

Made in the USA
Lexington, KY
06 January 2011